T0197387

HANNAH LOVES VERBS

Verbs
for
Grades K-2

LILLIE OYEBANJO

To order additional copies of this book, contact:
Xlibris
844-714-8691
www.Xlibris.com
Orders@Xlibris.com

ISBN: Softcover   978-1-6641-1105-9
         EBook   978-1-6641-1104-2

Print information available on the last page

Rev. date: 10/13/2021

HANNAH LOVES VERBS

Verbs Used

Eat   wash   dress   walk
write   talk   play   ride   hug

Hi, friends. I am Hannah.
I love **verbs**. I love **verb**s.
Verbs are things that
I can do. I can do.

In the morning, I eat breakfast.
Eat breakfast. Eat breakfast.
Eat is something I can do. I can do.
Eat is a **verb.** Eat is a **verb.**
I can eat, so eat is a **verb**.

After that,
I wash my plate. Wash my plate.
Wash is something I can do. I can do.
Wash is a **verb**. Wash is a **verb**.
I can wash, so wash is a **verb**.

Next,
I dress myself. Dress myself.
Dress is something I can do. I can do.
Dress is a **verb.** Dress is a **verb**.
I can dress, so dress is a **verb**.

Later on,
I walk to school. Walk to school.
Walk is something I can do. I can do.
Walk is a **verb**. Walk is a **verb**.
I can walk, so walk is a **verb.**

In class,
I write my name. Write my name.
Write is something I can do. I can do.
Write is a **verb**. Write is a **verb**.
I can write, so write is a **verb**.

At lunch,
I talk to friends. Talk to friends.
Talk is something I can do. I can do.
Talk is a **verb**. Talk is a **verb**.
I can talk, so talk is a **verb**.

At recess,
I play ball. I play ball.
Play is something I can do. I can do.
Play is a **verb.** Play is a **verb.**
I can play, so play is a **verb.**

After school,
I ride the bus. Ride the bus.
Ride is something I can do. I can do.
Ride is a **verb.** Ride is a **verb.**
I can ride, so ride is a **verb.**

When I get home,
I hug my mom. Hug my dad.
Hug is something I can do. I can do.
Hug is a **verb.** Hug is a **verb.**
I can hug, so hug is a **verb.**

I can eat.

I can wash.

These are things that I can do.

Eat and *wash* are **verbs**.

I can dress.
I can walk.
These are things that I can do.
Dress and *walk* are **verbs**.

I can write.

I can talk.

These are things that I can do.

Write and *talk* are **verbs**.

I can play.
I can ride.
I can hug.
These are things that I can do.
Play, *ride*, and *hug* are **verbs.**

Now, it's your turn.

Do you have things that you can do?
You can do?
Now write some things that you can do.
You can do.

I can_____. I can_____.

I can_____. I can_____.

I can_____. I can_____.

I can_____. I can_____.

I can_____. I can_____.

Write some **verbs**.
Write some **verbs.**

_____   _____

_____   _____

_____   _____

_____   _____

_____   _____

Printed in the United States
by Baker & Taylor Publisher Services